ISBN 978-1-330-80207-6
PIBN 10107314

1 MONTH OF FREE READING

at

www.ForgottenBooks.com

By purchasing this book you are eligible for one month membership to ForgottenBooks.com, giving you unlimited access to our entire collection of over 700,000 titles via our web site and mobile apps.

To claim your free month visit:
www.forgottenbooks.com/free107314

Similar Books Are Available from
www.forgottenbooks.com

PHILOSOPHIC SERIES—No. IV.

CERTITUDE, PROVIDENCE, AND PRAYER

BY

JAMES McCOSH, D.D., LL.D., D.L.

PRESIDENT OF PRINCETON COLLEGE

AUTHOR OF "METHOD OF DIVINE GOVERNMENT," "INTUITIONS,"
"LAWS OF DISCURSIVE THOUGHT," "EMOTIONS," ETC.

NEW YORK

CHARLES SCRIBNER'S SONS

1883

Trow's
PRINTING AND BOOKBINDING COMPANY
201-213 East Twelfth Street
NEW YORK

CONTENTS.

694439

CERTITUDE, PROVIDENCE AND PRAYER.

INTRODUCTION.

I AM accustomed to characterize the age as one of un-settled opinion; certainly not one of strong faith, nor yet of avowed scepticism, but of restless creed. There is a wide-spread impression that the advance of thought, and especially of natural science, has undermined old and fundamental truths both in philosophy and religion. I am endeavoring to show in this series of papers that it is not so. Some of these truths may have to be put in a new and more correct form; the defence of them has to proceed in a wiser way; but the radical principle remains as deeply and firmly established as ever.

The doubts and difficulties issue from four quarters of the heavens, or rather of the clouds.

I. From philosophy or metaphysics. There is a growing idea that all truth is drawn from experience, that innate ideas are dead and committed to the grave, from which it would be offensive to raise them, and that their heirs and successors, *à priori* principles, are waxing old and are ready to perish. If this be so, there is left to us no universal or even positive truth, certainly no eternal or absolute truth, as the experience of the individual and of the race must be limited; it can give us only knowledge

produced by circumstances, and which may change with circumstances and vary with the position.   The issue of the
uncertainty is agnosticism logically, and scepticism chrono-
logically—that is, when the causes have time to work.   I
have met and faced this error in No. I. of this series,
and mean to give point and application to my reply in this
number.   I do so by a more sober account than is usually
given of first, or *à priori* truths.   I have to defend my
position by examining historically, in future numbers, the
opinions of such influential thinkers as Locke, Berkeley,
Hume, Kant, and Herbert Spencer, and endeavoring to
find out what truth they held, and what the errors into
which they fell.

II. From natural science.   It is alleged that all nature,
physical and psychical, can be accounted for by cause
and law and development, which are shown to prevail
universally.   The mistakes thus arising I have endeavored
to expose in No. II. of this series, where I have sought to
clear up the subject of cause; and in No. III., where I have
shown that development is an organized causation having
a wide field, but at the same time decided limits, and
being simply a method by which God works.

III. From ethics.   There is an attempt made to de-
velop conscience and morality from experience and from
heredity.   It is allowed that this makes good and evil depend on circumstances, and makes it possible that the
good in one world may be evil in another, and the evil in
one constitution of external things be good in a different
state of things.   It is to be met by showing that there is
a morality which does not shift, but is in the very nature
of things.   This subject will be taken up in this number,
and will be more fully discussed in the criticism of Herbert Spencer's system as culminated in his "Ethics."

IV. From cosmogony.   As the result of all these diseussions there are doubts as to what is the nature of our world. Is it optimist or pessimist ? the best possible or the worst possible ? or neither ? This brings before us Providence and Prayer, and it will be shown that this world is not the best, for it has evil, nor the worst, for it has plenteous good ; it is a world not perfect, but going on toward perfection. This topic is started in this number, and will come up once and again for discussion and settlement.

SECTION I.

REALISM AND CERTAINTY.

Common people, and even thinking people, are not much inclined to speculate, or so much as to inquire, as to the actuality and certainty which they hold by. They assume certain obvious realities, and are sure that they know them, and they do not wish to be disturbed by thinking on these points, say as to their own existence or that of their mother, and are rather irritated when doubts are raised or they are subjected to questionings. But when puzzling thoughts arise, and objections are urged, and they are compelled to reflect and to speculate, they have then to face the question, is there a reality and can we find it ?

The search of the Eleatics, the earliest Greek metaphysicians, was for reality—τὸ ὄν and τὸ εἶναι.[1] They saw that the popular apprehensions were often erroneous, and they

---

[1] The Greek phrase τὸ ὄν is often translated absolute in the German histories of philosophy. But absolute is rather a modern idea, stirred up by the theological belief as to infinity, and metaphysical discussions as to conditions. The Greek inquiry was after realities as distinguished from appearances.

labored to correct them by finding what things exactly
are, and they came down to what is fixed and unchangeable.   This was also the main aim of Plato, who sought
by a subtle dialectic, and by bringing in an Idea, to reconcile the opposing systems of his day, and the fixedness
of things with their changing appearances.   The search,
openly or correctly, has a deep place in the whole Greek
philosophy, even in that of Aristotle, who did more than
any other to bring down philosophy to facts, while its own
region is above facts.   The fault of the subtle specu-
lators was that they dived down to the bottom of the well
to find the pure water which had risen to the surface, and
in doing so they stirred up mud which troubled the whole.

Modern metaphysicians have been disposed to make our
conviction as to reality to be the result of a complex process, which they had to unfold.   Descartes made the
knowledge of self take the form, if not the reality, of
reasoning : *Cogito, ergo sum.*   Descartes and Locke both
represent the mind as knowing and looking at an idea
in the mind, or out of the mind, instead of matter itself.
Berkeley, adopting this principle, showed that we have
no proof of the existence of matter.   Hume drove the
philosophy of his day to its logical consequences, and
beginning only with "impressions" and "ideas," without a thing to impress the mind, or a mind to impress,
landed thinking in universal scepticism.   Even Reid did
not speak very decidedly about self-consciousness as perceiving self directly, and he talks of sensations "suggest-
ing" the perception of an external world.   In arguing
with the sceptic Kant was unwilling to postulate too much,
and he started with presentations unknown, or with phenomena in the sense of appearances, and not with things ;
and he could reach reality only by a process which his
greatest admirers regard as unsatisfactory, and which, it is

now argued, issues logically in agnosticism. Hegel, to his credit, tried to bring back thought to reality, but it is by a dialectic process, which, as it did not begin with reality, never could reach it by legitimate logical inference, or rise higher than the subjective process.

It is time now to return to the natural method, and to avow it and justify it. In reflective as in spontaneous thought, in metaphysical philosophy as in natural thinking and conviction, we should start with existing things. Let us commence with our own existence, that is, with self as existing, always along with something affecting it. There is no intellectual or moral impulse, no felt want or desideratum of any kind requiring us to prove our own existence. We need not try to prove it. If we try, it will only be to find that we cannot; for there is nothing simpler or more evident from which to infer it. We should at the same time begin with the existence of external and material objects as affecting us. It is conceivable indeed that this step is a derivative one. It is urged by some that, knowing self, we may by a process reach a something out of self, and extended, that is, occupying space. But this process, if there be such, must be instinctive. We cannot by reasoning, or any legitimate discursive step, leap over the chasm between the self and the not self, any more than we can leap over our own shadow. We apprehend body as extended, but there is nothing in an unextended self to entitle us thence to infer an external and extended object. Just as little can this be done by a gathered experience, for when externality and extension are not in any one of the experiences we cannot find them in an accumulation of them. Altogether it is the most satisfactory hypothesis to assume the existence both of a self and an extended not self. No, it is not an hypothesis, it is a fact that we know both.

But it is objected, Do you hold, and justify yourself in holding, what cannot be proven? To this I reply that there may be two kinds of evidence, one immediate and the other mediate. When I open my eyes on a letter I know that there is a colored surface before me; I do not need evidence through anything else, for I have it in the thing itself; it is self-evident. But when I argue that this is a letter from a friend, I need mediate evidence, say in the signature attached. The mind does not insist on having indirect light, we may have direct. It is sure that the direct evidence, when it can be had, is the more satisfactory. It demands immediate proof only when it has not the other. In all cases the mediate proof proceeds in the end on an immediate proof on which it depends. There is a primitive knowledge anterior to and above mediate probation. It is so far a weakness in us that we are not able to know a thing directly, and to call in intermediate steps. We may believe that there are angelic beings who perceive things and truths at once, and without a process. We are not required to believe without evidence; but the evidence may be in the thing itself, that is, be self-evident.

But are we at liberty to appeal to assumed truths when we find it convenient, and thus render all probation and investigation unnecessary? Those who have used first principles have commonly enunciated tests—often, I admit, loosely stated. The test of necessity used by Leibnitz and Kant is the one most commonly appealed to in the present day—and it is decisive. It is the only criterion available to those who do not allow that we can perceive objects directly; but it is felt to be somewhat harsh to insist on us believing a proposition simply because we must do so. Those of us who hold that we can perceive objects directly have a prior and more satisfactory test—that of Self-Evidence; we know a thing, and are thus sure that it exists. As knowing it we cannot be made to think otherwise, and thus the secondary test, Necessity. These are confirmed by the third test, that of Catholicity, when we find the truth believed by all men.

But, it is asked, If first truths be so certain, how is it that there is so much uncertainty in the metaphysics which treat of them? In order to meet this question we have to draw two distinctions, which have been very much over-looked in speculative philosophy.

First, we have to distinguish between first truths, prop-erly so called, and other things—impressions, inferences, experiences—mixed with them. We can stand up confi-dently for the certainty of all original perceptions, but not for the rash reasonings upon them, or the feelings they gather around them. Our constitution, and the God who gave us our constitution, are not responsible for all the pretentious metaphysical principles which multitudes in-dulge in.

But there is a more important distinction. These first truths are all in the first instance singular. The child, the savage has certainly not before him general metaphysical principles, such as that it is impossible for the same thing to be and not to be at the same time. He simply knows that if a thing be here now, it cannot be elsewhere. He has not consciously before him the rule that the shortest distance between two points is a straight line; but he actually takes the straight line when he has to walk from one place to another. He is not in the way of conceiving or enunciat-ing the law that every effect has a cause; but on noticing a new thing, or a change on an old thing, he looks for a cause. It is only the mature man, only, in fact, the meta-physician, who is at pains to generalize or formulize the individual perceptions into a general law or axiom.

In doing this he may commit a mistake.   He may lay it
down as an indisputable principle, that "it is impossible for
the same thing to be and not to be," to find it contradicted
by the fact that a tree or a man exists now, and is gone in
a short time after ; and so he has to add the clause, "at the
same time."   Some one lays down the maxim that everything has a cause, and he is immediately asked has God a
cause, when he has to amend his statement, and make it
everything that begins to be has a cause.   The forming of
the general rule out of the individual and often complex
exercise of our primitive perceptions is one of the most
difficult tasks in which the human intellect can be engaged,
requiring the most careful observation and the sharpest sub-
tlety to disentangle the primitive truths from its accretions.
Confused statements, premature generalizations, and hasty
inferences abound in speculative philosophy more than in
any other branch of inquiry.   Metaphysics is commonly believed to be the most dubious and perplexed of all departments of science.   This is not because of any uncertainty
in the principles in the mind, but because of the difficulty
in apprehending and enunciating them.   The remedy is to
be found in insisting that those who use for any purpose a
first truth, which they assume without proving, should put
that truth (as is done in mathematics) in proper form and
show that it is in the mind.

Upon the primitive cognitions are reared other first
truths.   In Primitive Cognitions the object is present.
But we are quite as sure of the existence of other things
not present, as, for example, our conviction of our existence
in time past, and generally our convictions as to time, as
that time is continuous, and that all events are in time.
These constitute our Primitive Beliefs.   Again, in compar-
ing things known to us we discover at once that they agree
or do not agree.   These are Primitive Judgments.   It is

thus we decide that we are the same persons to-day that we were yesterday; that the whole is equal to the sum of its parts; that whatever is true of a class is true of each of the members of a class; that two parallel lines cannot meet; that time flows on; that equals added to equals are equals; that a property implies a substance, and an effect a cause.

So much for first truths. But by far the greater number of the truths which we are required to believe from day to day and from hour to hour are derivative. If we follow these sufficiently far down, we find they have a foundation firm and strong in first truths. But the derivative truths constitute a superstructure raised above them, and we have to see that all the parts be secure. We have now, I believe, convenient tests of these. There is truth gained by reasoning of which we have tests in the syllogism. There are general laws, reached by gathering facts, and we have now canons determining their validity. Some of them are certain, in fact, as certain as primitive truths, though not determined by the same kind of evidence. Others are only probable, but it may be so probable as to demand our assent, as that the sun will rise to-morrow; others may be doubtful, as that the planets are inhabited. The tests we have given in Series No. I. should determine the degree of probability. I have shown that among these primitive perceptions we have that of power and cause and effect, the precise nature of the energy being determined by experience (see No. II.). I have shown that causation leads to development, and that the development in the world is an organized causation accomplishing ends (see No. III.).

But has not evolution changed all this?

SECTION II.

EVOLUTION AND CERTITUDE.

It is certain that intelligence grows. The way in which it does is an instructive illustration of the nature of development. It is within ourselves, and we can see its workings in this department more readily than in any other.

It is always to be presupposed that there is an intelligent mind with capacities; without this presupposition we cannot advance a step. It is of the nature of these capacities to work. As they do so they are acquiring, accumulating, and combining knowledge. The child gets information by direct observation, and from parents, nurses, and teachers. As the boy advances in life he is ever noticing new facts, treasuring them up in the memory; is ever reflecting on them, arranging them, and subjecting them to abstraction, generalization, and reasoning. The brain grows by the exercise of the mind; the cerebral hemispheres of the mature man are larger than those of the infant; and those of civilized men, as a whole, weigh more than those of savages. It may be allowed, I think, that the mental capacities grow with the growth of the brain, that they both grow by mutual action, and that the mind itself is strengthened and enlarged by exercise, and by increase of knowledge.

So much for the growth of the individual. Now it will surely be allowed that this growth, or development if you choose to call it, does not destroy or set aside the primary intelligence; on the contrary, it enlarges it. The child acquires knowledge, and is ever adding to it. The later knowledge surely does not disannul the early. The growth, in fact, consists mainly in an increase of capacity to attain higher knowledge. True, the boy may be led to entertain narrow, or even erroneous opinions, but the mature man may correct them.

Herbert Spencer has been showing that not only is there a growth of the individual, but of the animal race. The attainments of one age go down by heredity to the succeeding one. The power of hunting acquired by the dog goes down to its descendants. Mr. Spencer holds that intelligence does thus go down from father or mother to son or daughter. It may be so. The brain structure determined by the habits of a parent may, by inheritance, determine a certain disposition in the children. But all this does not destroy, or even lessen, the capacity for acquiring knowledge. I can conceive a heredity that would bear down and crush all independence of thought, and place all mankind in the position of lunatics. But the actual heredity makes, or rather finds us, sane men, and increases our power of judging for ourselves.

The capacities which descend are perceptions of things. Heredity does not destroy human intelligence or render it untrustworthy. Every man has a power of knowing realities, and of distinguishing between truth and error. No matter how this power may have come, it may have been handed down by father or mother, or from grandfather and grandmother, or from a long line of ancestors, but it is the man's own; he may trust in it, and he is responsible for the use of it. In whatever way the intelligence may have been produced he can trust in it when it declares, upon the evidence furnished, that such an object, say a friend, exists; that such an event, say his marriage, has happened; and that mathematical truths, such as that all the angles of a triangle are together equal to two right angles, are certain. I am sure that there was such a man as Julius Cæsar; that there is such a city as Rome, and that the sun attracts the moon; and this, whether I did, or did not get the capacity to do so from my ancestors. A traveller sets out on a journey with a capacity to observe, and as he proceeds he is acquiring knowledge and increasing his acquisitions. The new ones do not set aside the old, they only add to them; and the addition may often clear up difficulties and correct wrong impressions, produced without evidence, as to the paths and boundaries of plain, bay, and forest. So it is with our capacities, hereditary or personal, they merely add to our powers of vision and enable us to discover further truth.

SECTION III.

EVOLUTION AND MORALITY.

Our moral power grows, just as intelligence does. Our ethical perceptions depend so far on our intelligence, as we must know what the deeds are, and what the motives of the actors, before we pronounce a sentence upon them, and this we have to do by our cognitive powers. Our moral powers thus grow with our powers of understanding. Not only so, but it may be allowed that the conscience grows by being properly exercised; it gathers by accretion, and becomes quicker in discernment. It is strengthened by the resistance it offers to evil, waxes valiant in the fight, and is made more confident and courageous by the victories it gains. As it looks to God and his law—the law of love—its vision is purified, its views are enlarged, and the sphere of duty is widened.

According to a prevalent philosophy in the present day, the conscience is a growth—a growth produced by circumstances. In other worlds our evil may be good and our good evil, or there may be no good and no evil. The idea of good thus becomes the product of position and events. This principle is implied covertly in utilitarianism. An action is good only so far as it produces pleasure, evil only so far as it leads to pain, and this depends on the surroundings. But conscience is not the product of circumstances any more than the intelligence is. Both are so far swayed by circumstances, but both have an independent power quite as much as the circumstances which sway them. I know that the opposite angles made by the intersection of two straight lines are equal to one another; and I know that charity, and sacrifice in a good cause, and speaking the truth are good, and that lying and hypocrisy are evil and only evil.

The idea of virtue being a product lies deepest down in the biological utilitarianism of Herbert Spencer. Virtue is the quality that produces pleasure, determined by a long succession of ages, and consolidated by heredity. Now it is true that our moral power grows, but it is growth from a germ. The faculty admits of improvement, but it is because it exists as a faculty. Love and justice are discerned as good in themselves—and not because of good consequences which follow from them because they are good—just as gold is seen to glitter. Ingratitude for favors and evil-speaking are seen to be evil in themselves, not because they lead to painful issues, which in fact follow because the deeds are evil, just as night is seen to be dark. Our conscience is of the nature of a perceptive power, looking at voluntary acts and perceiving them to be good or evil. We are as sure that mercy is a virtue as that the moon shines up there in the sky. We are as sure that murder is an evil as that poison kills. It matters not whether my perceptions have descended from my father or mother; they are now mine, quite as much so as my ocular vision, which, in like manner, has come to me by inheritance. It thus appears that development cannot interfere with the certitude either of truth or moral goodness.[1]

SECTION IV.

PROVIDENCE.

I am afraid that there is a growing number of people, who, while they believe in the existence and in the goodness of God, do not see him as they ought in the arrangements which he has made for the good of his creatures. This is one of the ways in which religion is losing its hold on the minds of thinking young men, who have been trained by science to discover causation and law in every part of nature. I fear there is not the same belief in providence as our forefathers held and cherished. In the theosophies of the East a divine power was seen and acknowledged in all the activity perceived in the universe; I have to add, however, without God being separated from his works. In Greece and Rome the people saw their different gods in the varied departments of nature: Jupiter in the thunder, Neptune in the waves, and Ceres in the crops. Our Christian forefathers delighted to discover God's hand in every event, which they believed to have a meaning which they diligently sought to ascertain. This was often done presumptuously and superstitiously. People argued a purpose and an end which the God who ordered the

---

[1] This subject will be more fully discussed in the paper on Herbert Spencer.

occurrences never saw, and interpreted events with a favoritism toward themselves and as judgments upon others. There is now a reaction against this whole style of sentiment, and people go to the opposite extreme, and regard it as vain to seek for a meaning in any of the operations of nature. There is a temptation here, fostered by the scientific spirit of the age, which believes in law and believes in development. Those who yield to this prevalent feeling lose many valuable lessons which God is teaching, if people would but observe his ways. I believe as firmly as any man can in the universality of law, and in the prevalence of development; but I regard them as processes by which God fulfils his purposes.

There is a GENERAL PROVIDENCE. God has so constituted his creatures that they have wants to be supplied, and he has made provision for supplying these. He sheds rain and sunshine upon the evil and the good. This is not effected by the mere powers of matter. These, if undirected, might work only confusion and mischief. Gravitation will pull down an imperfectly supported building upon our heads, and electricity, in the form of lightning, may destroy us on the instant. The potencies of nature, its mechanical powers, its chemical attractions, and its vital agencies are so arranged as to produce beneficent ends. But they have been so arranged, by him who formed them and acts in them; that they produce general laws which his intelligent creatures may observe, and to which they may accommodate themselves. It is seen very clearly in the revolving seasons of the year and in the periods in the life of animated beings—in their germination, their growth, their decay, and dissolution. Man can come to know these laws, and is expected to suit himself to them and take advantage of them. Nature does not provide for all our necessities without our requiring to exert ourselves;

this would tend only to produce idleness and self-conse-
quence, with all their attendant evils. In order to get
what he needs, man is obliged to be active and industrious,
and being so he secures blessings, always by the providence
which God has arranged so skilfully and beneficently.
The great body of mankind, all indeed except atheists, are
disposed to believe this, and are encouraged and com-
forted as they discover that the good and wise God has
planned it all.

So much all people, with a few exceptions, will be inclined to see and acknowledge, and as they do so a vague
feeling of reverence and love will rise up in their bosoms.
But there is a deeper meaning than this in the system of
nature.

There is a SPECIAL PROVIDENCE. The chief of a government, the general of an army, the head of a great mer-
cantile house have to satisfy themselves with giving
general orders which may be for the good of their de-
pendents, but they cannot anticipate every incident or
provide for the case of every individual. This is because
of the limited nature of their capacities and of their
knowledge. But no such weakness is laid on the Omni-
present One, who is in every place; on the Omniscient One,
who knows all things; and the Omnipotent, with whom
nothing is impossible. Every thing that falls out is appointed by him, nothing can occur unforeseen by him, and
no opposing power can thwart his will. Every man's lot,
and every incident in it, large or minute, prosperous or ad-
verse, successful or disappointing, is ordained and secured.
This is the doctrine of the greatest of all teachers, and is
the only one consistent with an enlarged conception of
God. " A sparrow cannot fall to the ground without
him." " The very hairs of our head are all numbered."
This was also taught by the wisest man of the most culti-

vated people of the ancient world : Socrates delighted to
see a purpose in every organ of our bodily frame, and
divine power watching over him and directing him in every
turn of his life. The Christian knows that his destiny
throughout is ordered by One who sees the end from the
beginning, and who cannot err or fall short in wisdom or
goodness, and who now sends this trial to warn, arrest,
and chastise, and anon bestows this gift for encouragement and comfort.

We can see a way in which God can accomplish special ends, and this in entire accordance with the prevalence
of law. In order to understand this it is necessary to re-
fer to the distinction stated briefly by Paley in the opening of his Natural Theology, expounded by Chalmers and
defended by Mr. J. S. Mill : it is the distinction between
the laws of matter and the collocations of matter ; or, as I
express it, between the powers and properties, on the one
hand, and the dispositions and arrangements of matter on
the other. Arrangements are evidently needed to make
the properties of matter work orderly and beneficently.
This is quite as certain as that there are laws or causes in
nature. In the construction of a building a great many
materials are brought together, and disposed according to
a plan, and to enable the edifice to fulfil its end. So it is
in that grand temple of nature which God has built. Its
separate objects, with their properties, are so disposed that
we have first a general order—a house with compartments
fitted for all, constituting that general providence of which
I have been speaking, such as the blessings secured by the
seasons. But farther, these dispositions are so made that
there is a place for each man, a provision for him, a guar-
dianship over him, and a course for him to pursue.

By this pre-arrangement God makes blind, mechanical,
chemical, and vital laws fulfil his benevolent and righteous

purposes. By this collocation rings inflexible in themselves are made flexible, and the fabric fits into the frame, covers it as a disc, and protects it as a coat of mail. The two, the general and the special providence, do not oppose or contradict each; they conspire and co-operate. There is no inconsistency, even in appearance, between God working everywhere in nature and the prevalence of physical causes and laws. God accomplishes individual ends by causes, and according to laws which he has appointed.

A stone will fall to the ground if unsupported, and this by a law which cannot be changed; but when it is falling from a high elevation, and might kill the person beneath it, another individual who is standing by turns it aside, and no injury is done. We say, and I think very properly, that all this is done by the providence of God, who gave to the stone its properties and place, and to the bystander his generous impulse.

But what are we to make of those dispensations which bring suffering and sorrow? Are we to regard them simply as casualties or fatalities? Or are we not rather to look upon them as judgments and as punishments? In seeking to answer such questions there is need of much thought and much charity. We have warnings on this subject from very high authority. One of the lessons taught by the grand dialogues in the Book of Job is that we are, not to regard suffering as proving the existence of special sin. The Great Teacher warns us, " Suppose ye that these Galileans were sinners above all the Galileans because they suffered such things? I tell you nay; but except ye repent ye shall all likewise perish. Or those eighteen upon whom the tower in Siloam fell, and slew them, think ye that they were sinners above all men that dwelt at Jerusalem? I tell you nay; but except ye repent ye shall all likewise perish."

There is a meaning in the afflictions which God sends, and we should seek to find what it is. There are cases in which we should discover in them the judgments of heaven.

1. We may discover God's judgments when the evil comes as the direct consequence of sin. There is no want of charity or kindness involved when we think and declare that this weakness or disease has sprung from vice, say from intemperance or loose living. When we can prove that the sins have been committed, we may and ought to observe that cunning and deceit deprive those who are guilty of them of the confidence of their fellow-men. We cannot and should not help experiencing a feeling of satisfaction when the wicked are caught in the trap they have laid for others. In all such cases indignation is a virtue, and the expression of it tends to purify the moral atmosphere in the community. There is a simpering charity which is a positive sin when it leads us to excuse or palliate known evil. God is speaking to us in all these judgments, and we should listen and stand in awe.

This is all we are entitled to do when the judgment is seen descending on others. But when a trying dispensation, say disease or disappointment, visits ourselves we may learn further and more special lessons. In such cases we may and always should inquire reverently what is its meaning to us. As we do so, we may not be able to discover at the moment all the ends which it is intended to serve; but still we may find out some of them. In all cases we should feel that we may profit by what God sends, and this whether we are able to decide for certain that God thus intended it; the fact that God has sent it is a presumption that he has a meaning in it. From our propinquity and close access to ourselves we may find that the event has a special direction toward us which others are

not able or entitled to notice. Even in regard to others
we may quietly observe, exercising charity all the while,
that a cross is sent at a particular time in order to correct and restrain a weakness or an evil in the character.
Thus a friend of mine much engrossed with public benevolent work, with very little time left for his family,
was laid aside from his labors by a malady which compelled him to live with his children, who were greatly
benefited thereby, and I saw a providence in it. We are
to be cautious in interpreting such occurrences in regard
to others; but we may often perceive the end to be accomplished in regard to ourselves. We are not entitled,
because events are all favoring us, to allow the impression
to spring up in our minds, that therefore we are the favorites
of heaven. Because a course followed by us is prospering,
we are not therefore to conclude that it has the approval
of God. It is not God's providence, as has often been
remarked, but his law which is to be the guide of life.
We must see beforehand that every step we take has the
approval of God; but having done so, we may notice as we
advance that God is encouraging us by the aid he gives,
by removing obstacles out of the way, and opening a path
through difficulties and perplexities. In particular we
may observe that a check is often laid upon us to keep us
from entering on a path where we might be exposed to
temptations which we are not able to resist. The good
man, as he walks on, will see that his steps are ordered by
the Lord. The aged man, in looking back on his past life
may discover that God has led him in a wonderful way,
such, it may be, as he did not wish, but which he now
sees to be full of wisdom, turning him aside when he was
entering upon a dangerous path, and opening a road for his
relief when he was shut in; restraining him when he was
advancing too rapidly, and stimulating him when he was

becoming slothful and discouraged. What he knows not now he will know hereafter, if not sooner, in the light of heaven.

I maintain that there is nothing in the most advanced discoveries of science to deprive any one of these consolations. The language of Bacon cannot be too frequently quoted: " It is true that a little philosophy inclineth man's mind to atheism, but depth in philosophy bringeth men's mind back to religion. For while the man looketh upon second causes scattered, it may sometimes rest in them and go no further; but when it beholdeth the chain of their confederate, and linked together, it must needs fly to Providence and Deity."

SECTION V.

PRAYER.

Here we presuppose that prayer is a duty, a duty to God and a duty to ourselves. We are constantly receiving gifts, and it is an obligation of common morality that we should thank the giver. We have his wondrous works spread out before us, and unless we sinfully restrain them. our hearts will prompt to praise. We daily commit sins, and we should daily confess them. We are always dependent on him, and it is meet that we should feel and acknowledge it. That man fails in one of the very highest ends of his existence who does not rise to communion with the great and good God. Such considerations, founded on the relation in which we stand toward our creator, preserver, and governor should lead us to pray, and we should allow no objections or cavils to tempt us to neglect or give up prayer, which is as clear a duty as any other binding upon us. Prayer is, in fact, a natural impulse, prompted by internal conscience and the feeling of gratitude, and called forth by the circumstances in which we are placed; and it is wrong in us, as some do, to resist it or seek to repress and crush it.

But does God hear and answer prayer? That he hears it we may argue from his omniscience. That he listens lovingly we may infer from his goodness and grace. But does he answer in the sense of granting our requests. Upon a Scotch minister, Dr. Leechman, publishing a sermon on the value of prayer as rendering the wishes it expresses more ardent and passionate, Hume remarked, " We can make use of no expression, or even thought, in prayers and entreaties which does not imply that these prayers have an influence." But there may be difficulties started as to the possibility of prayer being answered. I am not to enter into personal controversy, but the line of thought pursued in this part of my paper has reference throughout to an eminent physician in London, Sir John Richardson, who a few years ago proposed a Prayer Test, and to the objections taken by Professor Galton in his recently published " Inquiries into the Human Faculties."

The principal objection, the fundamental one, is that the laws of nature are fixed and unchangeable. The sun will rise at the appointed hour to-morrow, even though there be persons praying for certain ends of their own that he should not appear, or appear at a different hour. The tides will flow and ebb in order, even though those setting out on a voyage might wish, for their convenience and comfort, that they should not do so.

I have answered this objection in treating of Providence, of which the answer to prayer is an exemplification. God answers prayer by providence. God has arranged matter and its forces so that good purposes, small (as we reckon them) as well as great are accomplished; virtue is encouraged, vice is restrained, and among other good ends an answer is provided to the prayer of the most obscure believer, who is thus made to feel that he has not been overlooked in the plan of the universe. From the very beginning the prayer and its answer have been bound together in the counsels of heaven and the decrees of God. To accomplish his ends and to answer prayer it is not necessary that God should change his laws, for his unchanging laws may bring what is prayed for.

At this place I may call attention to two important principles fitted to stay and satisfy the mind. First, we have to take with us the doctrine of predestination, it being always so understood as to be compatible in itself, which it is, with the essential freedom of the will and the accountability of man. Indeed the modern doctrine of the uniformity of nature is substantially the same as that of foreordination, only seen under a somewhat different aspect—the one from below and the other from above, the one secular and the other spiritual, the latter being vastly the more comforting, as it brings in the will of a good God. In the ordination of nature, in the preordination of God, the prayer and its answer are so connected that the one follows the other, and without the one there would not be the other. This is one of the providential laws perfectly consistent with physical laws, and generally executed by physical laws.

We must take along with us another pleasant and consolatory truth, God acts in all the present actings of nature as really and truly as he acted in the beginning when he set nature agoing. God is as much present in his works as he ever was, and so when prayer is answered by natural agents it is answered by God quite as much as if answered by a visible hand or an audible voice, which are human rather than divine modes of communication and when used by God are, after all, mere physical means.

In order to explain all this, some have argued that time has no place in the apprehension of God. Some of the mediæval mystics spoke of God as an Eternal Now, and of past and the future being before him as much as the present. There is, it appears to me, a profound truth meant to be expressed in this statement. But it must not be so expressed as to make it contradict our intuitive knowledge of things. An eternal now, an eternal present, sounds very much like a contradiction. We perceive time to be a reality, that is, a thing existing. If it be so it must be known as a reality by God. But time may have quite a different relation to God to what it has to us. God is to be looked to and thought of as immediately present in his works when he made them, and now when they are acting. When man has constructed his machine he may leave it to itself to work, or rather he leaves it to God, who works in the natural agents. But God does not, and cannot from his nature, withdraw from the world and from acting in it when he has finished it. God is immanent in all his works in their first formation and in their continuance.

We need not trouble ourselves with the difficulty about God not being able to answer prayer, as everything has been fixed from the beginning. The difficulty arises from our narrow and anthropomorphic views of God. We must not transfer our weakness to the omnipotence of Deity. We must rather, in our imperfect manner, raise our conceptions to so high a sphere that God would be separated from human infirmities. God sees every existing thing at this instant. He does so every instant. Not only so, but I think he may be held as seeing every past instant and every future instant; in short, the whole past and future. Now this may be true, I believe it is so, of his love as well as of his knowledge. His love goes forth at this instant to every one of his creatures, just as the sun's rays go forth to every point of surrounding space. All this may be inconceivable to us, as to its mode of operation, but it is surely believable. But it may be that this love goes forth not only to all now existing creatures, it may go forth to all the past of living creatures, I am inclined to think also to all the future. We have some imperfect means of conceiving it, in the experience of human love, in the love of a mother interested in the past events of her son's life, and as she follows him on to the future. But the strongest human affections are limited. Not so with the love of God. It is expressively said, "Yea, I have loved thee with an everlasting love." Of old, from everlasting, his delights have been with the children of men. I apply this to prayer. We are apt to feel when God is said to have ordained the answer in the past ages of eternity as if this were removing God to an awful distance. But when God planned the answer he did it lovingly, and having in view our need and they earning of our hearts. When he actnally sends the answer it is under a like influence, he does so lovingly. When he grants the petition it is not against his will, or because he is compelled by his own decrees, but in thorough consonance with his will, lovingly and tenderly, it may be in pity.

[1] To the objection, Why then need I pray, since the answer is ordained? the reply is so stale that I am ashamed to be obliged to repeat it. It is an objection which may be taken to every form of activity. A man is in fever. He argues that, if it be predestined whether he is to recover, it is of no use sending for the physician.

---

[1] A considerable portion of this paper appeared in the *Independent* a few years ago when the Prayer Test was so discussed.

The answer is known to every tyro in moral science. If God has destined that the man recover, he may also have destined that he should send for the doctor. If he declines sending for the proper aid, he may find it destined that he is not to recover. So it is with the answer to prayer. If he prays, he may find that both the prayer and the answer are foreordained. If he neglect to pray, when in duty bound, he may find himself punished by being refused the blessing. In God's providence everything is carried on by means.

There are means that produce their end by direct natural agency. When a man sows, he may expect to reap. It does not need faith to show us this; a very short sight will enable us to perceive it. But there may be other means which bring about their end by the prearrangement of God, and not by physical power. And this is discerned only by that higher vision which is called faith; not that it is without reason, but because it is founded on a deeper insight into the character and ways of God. Dr. Tyndall tells us he is arguing against prayer as " a form of physical energy " (p. 764), as " a power in physical nature." I do not know what views may be taken of prayer in the scientific circles in which Dr. Tyndall moves, but I can say that I never met a religious man who claimed such a power for prayer.

No one praying in the right spirit believes that prayer has an influence on the wind, the rain, or health. Its power is over God, who planned all things at first, and acts in the rain, the wind, and the human frame. The God who prompts every grateful, every penitent heart to pray has connected the petition and the good it brings by ties as strong, though not so visible, as those which connect industry with its reward.

The mother prays for her sick child, and it is in answer

to her prayer that our physician comes in providentially with his remedy, suited to the constitution of the child, and the patient is relieved by physical laws, which are, however, subordinated to a higher provision, which the mother may believe in, but which the physician may not, even when he is made to accomplish the end designed.

He who prays in faith is falling in with the grand arrangements or laws (if you will) of the universe quite as much as he who sows in the hope of reaping. It is true, as Luther (quoted by our author) says, that *laborâsse est orâsse*, when it is labor for the glory of God and the good of man; but it is equally true *orâsse est laborâsse* in fulfilling the purposes of heaven.

A second objection is urged. Nobody believes that it is lawful to pray for every object—that it is lawful, for example, to pray that the earth should not move round the sun. "The phenomena of the universe are ranged by people who fully believe in the efficacy of petition in two categories; a class which I shall call Number One, respecting which it is quite useless, if not presumptuous, to pray, and a class, Number Two, of events, which are the legitimate objects of prayer. Now, it is curious to observe that there is no agreement at all among religious people as to the principles on which such a classification should be made" (p. 774). But pious people have a very clear rule for deciding all such cases. They pray for things agreeable to God's will. When God's will is intimated to them, no matter how, they will not pray against it. They will still pray, but their prayer now is that the event may be for good, and they be enabled to submit to it. When the boy is sick the pious mother prays that he may recover, if it be the will of God. When he dies she prays that she may be enabled to bear the trial in meekness and patience.

He hints plainly that the class of objects for which we can pray will grow less and less, and those for which we cannot pray will become more and more numerous. " The professed believer must follow, drawn by inexorable power, in the wake of advancing science, and after hard resistance, as always giving up one point after another, and resigning event after event, to be detached from the once great class of objects to be prayed for, and admitting their title of admission into the great class of settled and ordered events, not to be influenced by human interference, and capitulating with the best grace he may when forced to surrender." I admit that in a few, a very few, cases science may tell us what the will of God is before common observation can discover it. But the only effect of this is to change the prayer, " Do this, if it be thy will," a little sooner into the prayer, " Thy will be done."

And this tendency to lessen the number of objects to be prayed for is counteracted by another tendency brought into great prominence by modern science. Does not the latest science show that, as things advance, in time they become more and more complicated, and the issue is that wise men feel more their dependence on heaven? Does not M. Comte's famous classification of the sciences proceed on the principle of the complication of phenomena, and on the circumstance that phenomena become more and more complicated as we approach nearer to man, and becoming most complicated of all in human society? Has not physiology been showing that animals, as they rise in the scale, become more and more complex in their structure? Is not society, as it advances in knowledge and refinement, becoming more and more reticulated? And the greater the complexity the more difficult to foresee events and to find out what God has fixed. The most dependent of men is the great merchant or the great statesman, who has become involved with the trade of distant nations or the caprices of millions of human beings. Science can tell us what is and must be the tendency of a given force; but it cannot tell us what will be the result of an involved combination of forces. It can tell us where a satellite of Jupiter will be ten thousand years hence; but it cannot say whether his child will be dead or alive a day hence.

But after science has done its utmost, there will remain a vast and immeasurable domain in which, as God's will is not intimated, we may humbly make known our will, adding always, "Notwithstanding, not my will but thine be done." Dr. Tyndall treats us to a long account of religious men who have opposed science and been defeated—I may say justly defeated, as setting themselves against one way in which God makes known his will. But I could give a far longer list of men who have set themselves to oppose providence and prayer, only to find that, as Beza said, "God's word is an anvil which has worn out many a hammer."

It is urged that facts go to show that there is not an answer to prayer. It is proven that those most prayed for do not live longer than others. Kings and governors have usually had constant and numerous petitions put up in their behalf, and yet their lives are not prolonged beyond the average. Missionaries are prayed for by multitudes that they may be safely carried by sea and land to their fields of labor, and that they may there be spared for usefulness, and yet it does not appear that their voyages are more prosperous than those of others in the same circumstances or that they live to a greater age. Life insurances do not take a less premium from those who are specially prayed for than from those who are not. Looking to these things the physician proposed a Prayer Test. The patients on

one side of an hospital were to be prayed for and those on
the other side were not; and then it was to be determined
whether the former recovered while the others did not.
This seemed very dexterous. But surely God is not
thus to be mocked, and his praying people were not so
silly as to be taken in by so preposterous a proposal. It is
astonishing to find how ignorant many of our *savans*, deep
in the science of matter, are as to moral questions and the
evidence by which they are settled drawn from mind and
conscience and the obvious method of providence. It is
not by such an experiment that the father has to settle
how he has to train his son; that the earnest youth has to
determine how he should set out on the journey of life;
that the statesman has to fix on measures for promoting the
welfare of his country.

The very purpose of God in governing the world by
general laws is to secure that his intelligent creatures may
from the past anticipate the future, which they could not
do, were there no regular law or if this was disturbed by
constant interferences. We may be sure, then, that God
will not interfere with laws or regulations which he himself
has devised, so as to lessen foresight or disturb reasonable
expectations. We cannot conceive that God should so
order events as to help or hinder insurance companies. In
answering prayer God, humanly speaking, has to look to
and to weigh a great many considerations—that is, facts and
reasons which would have to be considered by man in like
circumstances. He has to act as wise parents have to do
in granting or refusing the request of their children. In
the answer to be given to his prayers every one who
knows himself will leave a discretion with God. It is
surely a happy thing for God's creatures that he does not
grant every one of their wishes. I do not know that those
who pray for kings expect them to live longer than other

men. Christians cannot consent, while they pray for some men, to bind themselves not to pray for others. They will not petulantly conclude that God does not hear or answer prayer because he has not allowed them all that they demanded. In the experience of years they will discover that God has been kind to them, even as their parents were in their childhood, in refusing them certain things which they earnestly wished to obtain.

Professor Galton thinks that if it were known that God answers prayer, insurance companies might take a lower premium from those that did pray, or were much prayed for. But every man of sense sees that the infinitely wise God could not be expected to fall in with such a mode of procedure, as it would only promote religious hypocrisy. There can be no doubt that good moral men live longer than others, but life insurance offices do not lessen their charges to suit the supposed character of the applicants; if they tried to do so they would fall into favoritism and perpetual mistakes ;—they have to satisfy themselves by excluding those whose known vices might injure their health and shorten their days. We can conceive of the wise God, who sends rain to the evil as well as to the good, acting on a like principle, or rather in a sovereign way of his own, so as to prevent the evils that would arise from the indiscriminate granting of petitions.

I assume that God is all-powerful, that he is all-wise, and that he is good. I hold by these truths on good and sufficient evidence notwithstanding that there is evil in the world. But it is clear that in dealing with man as possessed of free will and as having sinned, he must act on principles (if we can so speak) different from those on which we act, and which we may not be able to comprehend. For us to allow evil, which we have power to prevent, would be wrong, except, indeed, in circumstances in which we are not at liberty to interfere with the free will of the agent. But were God bound by any such obligation, it is clear that evil would not exist in the world. Altogether, God's ways are not, and cannot be, like our ways in all respects. Many of them, in their device and mode of execution, lie in a region altogether beyond our ken. We must believe, indeed, that in nature and kind justice with God, must be the same as justice with us. We cannot conceive that the wise and just God should act capriciously or arbitrarily, but he may, always in consistency with his character, act in a manner which we are not in a position to judge of.

What advantage, then, has the praying man? Much in every way. We pray as a duty, and it becomes pleasant. We unbosom ourselves to Him, and find that we have comfort in doing so. We confess our sins to God, and feel a relief as if we had thereby thrown off a load. We pray for the forgiveness of sins, and trust that God has delivered us from the guilt. We ask divine aid to enable us to resist the evil, and feel that we have got strength in the very act. We seek to have communion with God, and feel at times that we have succeeded. We do not address him as we would these lofty mountains and these stars which cannot reciprocate our feelings. We speak to him in the confidence that he is hearing us, and that he is speaking to us. We become like him as we look to him, as we have seen the image of heaven reflected on the bosom of a tranquil lake spread out beneath it. We pray in the certain belief that God hears us. We ask for temporal gifts so far as they may be agreeable to God's will, for our own higher good, and the good of others. We are sure that as God hears our prayers so he will answer them; but we do not dictate to Deity and prescribe to him what the answer shall be and how it must come. We pray for what God sees we need, and are sure it will be supplied. We pray most earnestly for spiritual blessings, knowing that these will always be agreeable to the will of God. As we thus hold intercourse with God our will becomes assimilated to the divine will, and we thank him for what he withholds as well as for what he grants.

A father encourages his child to make known his wishes, and lets him know that they will be attended to. This does not imply that every one of the petitions will be granted, even those that are capricious, or which the father knows might injure his boy. He complies with the entreaties, so far as this can be done consistently with the wise regulations of his household, so far as circumstances admit, and so far as the youth's best welfare is not interfered with. It is much the same with our heavenly father when we are assured that, "if men who are evil know how to give good things to their children, much more shall our heavenly father give good things to those who ask him." The two cases, indeed, that of our heavenly father and that of an earthly father, are not identical, but they are parallel, and the earthly may throw light on the beavenly. God, in his sovereign wisdom and for our good, has laid down governmental laws, and these he cannot be expected to contravene; and much as he may yearn to grant the requests of those who pray, yet he will not do so when this might injure their best interests; he will not, for instance, give them wealth when this might make them vain and proud, or tempt them into sinful indulgences.

SECTION VI.

WHAT IS OUR WORLD?

This is a question which thinking minds have been putting and pressing from the beginning. It is one asked with intense eagerness and earnestness in these our times when science is making so many discoveries, when the heavens are opening to us new wonders, more especially as to the identity of the composition of stars and earth, and when the life and growth of plants are giving us glimpses of the inner secrets of generation and heredity. We know what the experience of man says. We know what the Scriptures say. What does science say? Do these three testimonies conflict? or are they substantially the same? We are in the heart of a profound subject which philosophers like Kant dignify with the name of Cosmology when they represent all higher and deeper thought as clustering round Theology, Anthropology, and Cosmology.

I.

When we believe that this world is the workmanship of God, all-powerful and benevolent, our first idea is that there should be nothing in it but beauty and benignity. The youth setting out on the journey through it is apt to expect to find only health and happiness, peace and prosperity, sunshine and calm, flowers and fruit, love and smiles. There are abundance of such scenes on our earth's surface, and we should feel a pleasure in beholding them ; children prattling, young men and maidens romping, pure and happy homes, prosperous lives in which character and honesty are rewarded, and contented old age living on the earnings of industry and activity. This is the life which the youthful fancy paints, and which the fond mother wishes for her son. But other aspects press on our notice whether we wish it or not. If there be blue sky over our heads, it may soon be covered with clouds big with devastating torrents. If there be lovely landscapes on the earth, there are also howling deserts and malarial marshes. There is the light of day, but quite as lengthened is the darkness of night into which the day sinks. You see promising buds and blossoms, but how many are nipped by the frosts and blown away by the wind. The youth finishes his laborious education to find himself smitten down and his attainments' apparently lost. The father expects the son to help and sustain him through life, and at last to lay his head in the grave, but has instead to perform that duty to his son. That young man has to weep over the grave of one whom he expected to be his bride and his life-partner. The serpent with his slime and his sting crawls into our home, pleasant as Paradise, and we have to leave it, hurt and sorrowing. If there be high enjoyments in our world there are also temptations and sins polluting the waters and making them offensive. We have all seen the hope of his family and his friends led astray, and, as they hold down their heads in shame, they have to consign his remains to a dishonored grave. The drunken son is brought home to the house of his mother, who is thereby driven to a mad-house.

II.

It is a curious circumstance that later science seems to be exhibiting our world under the same double aspect. In my younger years *savans* enlarged admiringly, as well they

might, on the perfect order and beauty of the heavenly
bodies, and of the adaptation of all things to one another,
and of a good end in the plant and animal. One would have
thought that the world had come forth in the fulness of
perfection and as a good God might wish it. I remember
that I was not altogether satisfied with the account then
given of nature in college lectures and books of science.
I felt as if *prima facie* it was scarcely in consonance with
Scripture, and really inconsistent with our experience.
Scientific men showed us order and law as universally prevalent, and did not seem to think that there was anything
else. It was believed that the great French mathemati-
cians of the end of last century and the beginning of this,
had demonstrated that if this world were not interfered
with, it would go on forever. Paley had shown that there
was an evidently designed fitting of one organ to another
in every part of the animal frame.

But I could not but observe another order of facts with
a different look and expression. Everybody sees and feels,
and every candid man acknowledges, that there is evil in
our world as well as good. There is undoubtedly pleasure
in our world, but there is also pain, and the one is quite as
much a reality as the other. If there be happiness con-
tinned through years, there is also at times prolonged
misery. Law certainly reigns everywhere, but it seems
often to work blindly. The law of gravitation holds
a building firmly on its foundation, but it is quite as
ready to pull it down and murder those who are dwelling
in it. The fire that warms us may raise a conflagration
to wrap thousands in its flames. The elements which
unite to produce our food, may combine to produce poi-
sons. If there be pure air from heaven, there may also be
malarial damps from the earth. If there be widespread
health, there is also disease. You notice that mother,

to-day so happy as her eye follows that child who is play-
ing around her ; to-morrow that child is languishing on a
bed of distress, and next week has to be buried out of
sight.   To-day this man is strong, as if he were to live for
years; to-morrow he is stretched helpless on a bed of dis-·
tress, with no hope of ever rising.   This year there is an
unbroken family—father, mother, and children—next year
the children are orphans, cast upon the world's cold charity.
That young man has prepared himself at school, at college,
in the shop or factory, for honorable work, but is not allowed to enter upon it.   If there be multitudinous life, it
everywhere terminates in death.

There is a worse evil than pain, there is sin.   If we do
not purposely shut our eyes, we have to see it everywhere.
In every age and in every country there have been wars
and rumors of wars.   History has consisted very much in
the narrative of political strifes and bloody battles.   In
every great city there are sinks into which filth is constantly
pouring.   Even in our quietest rural districts, and our apparently happiest homes, are feuds and lusts breaking out
in crimes, in slanders, fights, divorces, and murders, which
startle the community.   We do not need to look to distant
places to discover all this, we find it close to us breaking
out in ourselves in evil words and deeds ; we feel it fester-
ing within us as a fever.   We need not, we cannot deny
it.   There is pain in our world, and this is an evil; there is
sin in our world, and this is a worse evil.

Later science has shown us that the worlds have been
formed as they now are in the course of long ages, in which
have been warring elements, convulsions with violent up-
heavals, with earthquakes, with volcanoes, with seas over-
whelming continents, and whole races perishing because
they have become unfitted to their new surroundings.
There is a dissipation of energy which in the end will

break up our world, and burn it with fire. It has been shown by geology that when animals were created capable of receiving pleasure, they were also liable to suffering and death. "A struggle for existence" is the characteristic of animated life from the beginning.

All this while there are everywhere order and care. The arguments of Paley and other writers on natural theology in behalf of the existence and benevolence of God are as strong as they ever were and were thought to be by our fathers. When we look to this crowning goodness we feel as if there is something unnatural in the evils which appear in our world. It looks as if creation were unwillingly subject to them. Nature seems to rebel against the evils that are in it. "For the creation was made subject to vanity, not willingly, but by reason of him who hath subjected the same in hope" The creation is striving against the tendency to evil. If there be diseases in our world there are also remedies. Nature everywhere seeks to restore itself. If there be winters in the succession of seasons, they are followed by springs, going on to summers and autumns. If there be the deaths of the individuals, there is the continuance of the race. If there be travailing, it is in order to a birth. If there be deaths there are also resurrections. Nature is struggling, but it is in order to improvement. It is ploughing in order to sow and reap in due season. All creation is moving onward, but also upward. There is a struggle for existence, but a certainty that in the end the good will gain the victory.

III.

In all this, science seems to be coming nearer to the account given in Scripture. Take only one passage: "For the earnest expectation of the creature waiteth for the manifestation of the sons of God. For the creature was made subject to vanity, not willingly, but by reason of him who hath subjected the same in hope. Because the creature (creation) itself also shall be delivered from the bondage of corruption into the glorious liberty of the children of God. For we know that the whole creation groaneth and travaileth in pain together until now." (Rom. viii., 19–23.) Socrates said of the philosophy of Heraclitus, "What I understand is so excellent that what I do not understand I am sure must also be excellent." I understand so much of this and other like passages, but I believe it contains depths of meaning which I cannot fathom. It opens to me glimpses of objects more remote than the stars and more glorious; of nebulæ which we may not be able to reduce, but which shine across our sky like the Milky Way with a mild lustre. There is evil, "vanity," "corruption," and "bondage," and a deep sense of the evil, "a groaning" and "travailing in pain;" but there is a "deliverance," "an earnest expectation," and "a waiting," and a "glorious liberty," and "manifestation" of restored sonship. This is the account in the Scripture of our world. I believe it to be given by inspired men. Some, indeed, may be disposed to argue that it is the product of the genius or reason of man; but if so, such views and sentiments must have come from the deepest heart of humanity, joining with experience and science to give their combined testimony as to the character of our world. Man craves for a deliverance and would fain look for a deliverance. He is conscious of the burden; he groans under it and cries for relief. The Scripture tells us who the deliverer is, and what the nature of his deliverance.

We see clearly that the work of deliverance must be a stupendous one, reaching over all creation if it is to be as wide as the evil. According to Scripture God accomplishes it in a particular way.   The deliverer says that "he must needs go up to Jerusalem and there suffer many things." When he said this Peter took him and began to rebuke him, saying, "Far be this from thee, Lord."   Our rationalists take the same view.   And yet there is a fitness and a propriety, in a world of suffering, that the deliverer himself should suffer.   God as God cannot suffer.   But he takes upon him our nature and has suffered and died.   God is love and he pities us.   God as God cannot have sympathy with us. But as having suffered he has a fellow-feeling with all our infirmities.   So we have the very remarkable expression that even Christ himself became "perfect through suffering," not perfected thereby in spiritual excellence, for he had been perfect from all eternity in holiness, but made perfect as our mediator and as having the human susceptibility of sympathy added to his divine love.

The reconciliation has many aspects.   There have been keen disputes among theologians as to the precise nature of the atonement.   These spring very much from the circumstance that some look upon it exclusively under one aspect, neglecting the others.   The essential feature of it seems to be that in it Christ suffers for us.   If we leave out this, we are leaving out the deepest principle in the transaction.   He had to say, "I have a baptism to be baptized with, and how am I straitened till it be accomplished." He "groaned in the spirit and was troubled" as he contemplated death at the grave of Lazarus.   In his agony in the garden he prayed, "if it be possible let this cup pass from me;" but it was not possible for it to pass if the deliverance was to be accomplished.   More mysterious still, he had to say ere he expired, "My God, my God, why hast thou forsaken me."   To this earnest appeal no answer was given. These heavens continued shut and silent.   "My God, my God, why hast thou forsaken me."   Let us come to the foot of the cross and give the answer. "Thou wert forsaken because of our sins. 'Surely he hath borne our griefs, and carried our sorrows: yet we did esteem him stricken, smitten of God, and afflicted. But he was wounded for our transgressions, he was bruised for our iniquities: the chastisement of our peace was upon him; and by his stripes we are healed.'"

This is the keystone of the arch. But there are other aspects which ought not to be overlooked. There is what is called the moral aspect. Herein God manifests his love, and yet upholds the integrity of his law. The sin is condemned and yet the sinner is saved. Farther, it is evident from this passage and from others that the rectification extends beyond our world. Science shows that every part of our cosmos is connected with every other. There is an attraction which binds all the bodies in one system. There are the same elements in distant stars as our earth. I move my arm, and an energy is let loose which may reach the most remote regions of space. It looks as if in like manner the restoration secured in Christ reaches over all creation. The earnest expectation of creation waiteth for the revealing or manifestation of the sons of God. The creation feels as if it should claim God as a father, and yet as if this fatherhood, through the evil, had been lost, and it looks for a restoration, for the revealing or manifestation of the sons of God. The grand reconciliation is effected by him who "made peace through the blood of his cross, by him to reconcile all things unto himself; by him, I say, whether they be things in earth, or things in heaven."

Such is our world as attested by three witnesses. All men have seen and felt the evil, and this whether they look at it seriously or not, whether they avow it or not. Some have viewed it with a growling malignity, and argued that its existence shows that there is no proof of God's existence. The ancient sceptics gloated over the disorders in our world, the earthquakes, famines, and pestilences, the failure of good men and the success of bad. As they looked at these things James Mill the father, and John Mill the son, concluded that if there be a God all-powerful and good he would not have permitted these things.

I am not here to enter on the subject of the origin of evil. In my younger years I tried once and again to solve the problem. In my later life I have given up the attempt. I have become convinced that no one has cleared up the mystery, which remains as the one dark cloud in our sky. The great German philosopher, Liebnitz, propounded a grand doctrine of optimism which asserts that this is the best possible world, and this doctrine was expounded with glowing eloquence by Bolingbroke and in terse verse by Pope. This style of sentiment prevailed in our literature for more than a century, and people did little to remove the evils in our world or to elevate the great mass of the people, many of whom sank in our great cities to the lowest depths of degradation. But in later times thinkers have been obliged to view the other aspects. Astronomy teaches the generation of worlds out of star dust. Geology tells us that death has reigned over all animated beings from the beginning. In all past ages there has been a struggle for existence. We have now pessimism, which declares that the world is the worst possible, proclaimed and defended by a few moodish men of genius, and youths are wondering at it, and finding a confirmation of it in the circumstance that they are not meeting with an encouragement suited to their merits and their opinion of themselves.

On two points I have reached assurance : one is that God is not and cannot be the author of evil, and on the other hand, that those intelligent creatures who commit sin are themselves to blame for it. Carrying these two convictions with me I leave speculative questions with God, of whose existence and goodness I have such abundant proof.

On one other point I have reached assurance: the existence of pain is not inconsistent with the existence of love. Suffering is one of the most potent means of calling forth love. The shepherd left the ninety and nine sheep in the wilderness to go after that which was lost. There was a tenderness in the interest which the father took in his returning prodigal son beyond what he felt in the one always with him, and which led him to run out to meet him and embrace him in his arms. "There is joy in heaven among the holy angels over one sinner that repenteth." "Pure religion, and undefiled before God and the Father, is this: To visit the fatherless and widows in their affliction, and to keep himself unspotted from the world." Man may feel at times as if he were kept at an infinite distance from God; yet if he would but think of it there is an endearing element in the love of God toward sinful men not found in his love to the holy angels. There is pity: "Like as a father pitieth his children, so the Lord pitieth them that fear him." That apparent frown which we see at times on the face of God is assumed only because God has to mark his disapprobation of our conduct; his love all the while being ready to burst out. Thus it was that God was led to give up his only begotten son to suffer and to die for us. It was this affection which led the Son to leave the bosom of the Father and suffer and die on earth. The highest exercise of love which the universe discloses is the love of God—Father, Son, and Holy Spirit—toward fallen and suffering man. "Herein indeed is love." The mystery of darkness is swallowed up in the mystery of light, as we "comprehend with all saints what is the breadth, and length, and depth, and height;

and to know the love of Christ, which passeth knowledge."

IV.

There are literary and scientific men in the present day who have outgrown, as they claim, the gospel; outgrown it as the man outgrows the clothes of his childhood, as the young plant bursts from the envelope that protected it. But what have they substituted? A skeleton with the living form stript off. Nothing, absolutely nothing to give peace, and life, and assurance. Thomas Carlyle, whom all persons of literary tastes are talking about in these times, when every feature of his strong but not very lovely character is exhibited to us, used to talk of the "eternities," "the infinitudes," the "realities," "the moralities," "the idealities." Matthew Arnold speaks of "sweetness and light," and "making for righteousness," things equally empty and inane. These at best are abstractions, not filling up or satisfying the heart, as they are without a living God and a loving Saviour. A younger set of men, their true offspring, have sprung up among us, and going on in the same direction have scattered and dissipated the empty truth retained in these generalities. Those who have given up Christ find that they have to give up God, and those who have given up God find that they have no sustaining morality left them; no peace, no hope of immortality.[1] "O Father, Lord of heaven and earth, thou hast hid these things from the wise and prudent, and hast revealed them unto babes. Even so, Father, for so it seemed good in my sight."

---

[1] Some years ago I had a call at my house, in Ireland, by a young nobleman with whom I was at that time intimate, and who has since risen to eminence as a statesman (I mean Earl Dufferin), who introduced to me his friend Lord Ashburton. The nobleman introduced took

What, then, is the conclusion to which we have come in our cosmology? Our world is not all good on the one hand, nor is it all evil on the other. In it by the capacities we possess and the opportunities afforded we can discover truth solid and satisfactory, but in which we may fall into error if our eye be not single. It is a world in which we know only in part, but in which we get glimpses of vastly more which we do not know. It is not a world at rest, but a world in perpetual activity, every atom and every mass in rapid and unceasing motion, proceeding by conflicting forces, but all in a regulated system. There is inflexible law, in which we can trust, and to which we can accommodate ourselves to secure ends, and yet a providence whereby it is made to take care of us and supply our

---

me aside and said, "You know that I have lately lost my dear wife, who was a great friend of Mr. Carlyle's, and I have applied to Mr. Carlyle to tell me what I should do to have peace, and make me what I should be. On my making this request he simply bade me read Goethe's Wilhelm Meister. I did so, and did not find anything there fitted to improve me. I went back to Mr. Carlyle, asking him what precise lesson he meant me to gather from the book, and he said 'Read Wilhelm Meister a second time.' I have done so earnestly, but I confess I am utterly unable to find any thing there to meet my anxiety, and I wish you, if you can, to explain what Mr. Carlyle could mean." I told him that I was not the man to explain Carlyle's meaning, if indeed he had any definite meaning. I told him plainly that neither Goethe nor Carlyle, though men of eminent literary genius, could supply the balm which his spirit needed ; and I remarked that Goethe's work contained not a little that was sensual. I did my best to point to a better way, and to the deliverance promised and secured in the gospel. I do not know the issue, but I got an eager listener. Carlyle wished to persuade his mother, a woman of simple but devoted piety, that his advanced faith was the same as that which she held firmly, and so much to her comfort, only in a somewhat different form. But in fact the mother's faith was crushed in the form in which the son put it, when it became a skeleton, as different from the life which sustained her as the bones in our museums are from the living animal.

special wants. It is a world in which God does not hold sensible communication with his creatures, but may be approached in prayer, which he will answer in his own way. In it we have a clear view of a moral law requiring obedience, but which we have disobeyed. There is evil in it, a universal evil—it is of no use denying this—but there is the universal hope of a deliverance. There has been a fall, but there has also been a recovery. God seems to have withdrawn, but by faith in the appointed mediator we can rise to communion with him. Our world is not perfect, but there is evidence that it is going on toward perfection. In it we are in a state of probation; if we stand it, it will issue in promotion to a higher sphere. Let us properly understand our position and conform to it.

PART I.

DIDACTIC.

In this part of the Series the principal philosophic questions of the day are discussed, including the Tests of Truth, Causation, Development, and the Character of our World.

No. I. CRITERIA OF DIVERSE KINDS OF TRUTH.

N B —This little volume might be used as a text-book in Colleges and Upper Schools

No II. ENERGY, EFFICIENT AND FINAL CAUSE. An attempt is here made to clear up the subject of Causation which has become considerably confused.

No III. DEVELOPMENT, WHAT IT CAN DO AND WHAT IT CANNOT DO. Development is here presented so as to show that it is not opposed to religion, and that the conclusions drawn from it by some of its defenders are not legitimate

No. IV. CERTITUDE, PROVIDENCE AND PRAYER with an inquiry as to what is the character of our world showing that it is neither optimist nor pessimist, but going on toward perfection.

N.B —There is an impression that later science and philosophy has set aside old and fundamental truths in religion and philosophy. It is not so. Some of the old truths may have to be put in a new form, and a new line of defence taken up, but the radical truths remain as deeply founded as ever.

PART II.

HISTORICAL.

In this part the same questions are treated historically. The systems of the philosophers who have discussed them are stated and examined, and the truth and error in each of them carefully pointed out.

No. V. LOCKE with a notice of BERKELEY. It is shown that Locke held by a body of truth, and that he has often been misunderstood ; but that he has not by his experience theory laid a sure foundation of knowledge.

No. VI. DAVID HUME as expounded by Huxley. It is necessary to examine Hume's scepticism, but it is best to do so in the defence of it by Huxley.

No VII. A CRITICISM OF THE CRITICAL PHILOSOPHY showing that Kant has stated and defended most important truths, but has undermined knowledge, by making the mind begin with appearances and not with things.

No. VIII. HERBERT SPENCER'S PHILOSOPHY as culminating in his Ethics Here there will be a careful examination of his physiological utilitarianism.

Each, one vol., 12mo, paper. Price, 50 cents.

*** NOTICE —Orders and subscriptions for the entire series will be received by

CHARLES SCRIBNER'S SONS, 743 & 745 BROADWAY, NEW YORK.

CPSIA information can be obtained
at www.ICGtesting.com
Printed in the USA
LVOW13s1446010217
522879LV00029B/950/P